SELECTED POEMS

DATE DUE

CONTENTS

PREFACE

There are a few people always in the world to stand for—to stand *up* for, I'd wanted to say—the possibilities of being human. If you look up the word, *poetry*, in a usual dictionary, you'll find it's something written by a poet. If you look up *poet*, you'll find it's someone who writes poetry. Mr. Dorn is such a poet, and his poems are so much the definition of what a poet can do, humanly, that my proposals here will be both brief and simple.

First of all, Charles Olson used to speak of Edward Dorn's *Elizabethan* care for the sound of syllables. That is, he was very respectful of this poet's ability to make every edge of the sound in words articulate. He didn't just go pounding along on the vowels, *o sole mio*, etc., he obviously enjoyed all the specific quality of sound that one could also make sing, e.g.,

> ... I don't
> want a rick of green wood, I told him
> I want cherry or alder or something strong
> and thin, or thick if dry, but I don't
> want the green wood, my wife would die ...

It's not easy to make "or alder" feel so comfortable a thing to say, and you'll see, or rather, hear, how he goes on playing this sound in the next line of this first poem here, an early one indeed.

Second, Mr. Dorn has always taken himself seriously, by which I mean he thought he, like all humans, counted for something. Years ago he told me a very moving story of how, the night of the graduation dance at the highschool he'd gone to in Villa Grove, Illinois, he and his date—she was wearing the classic white prom dress—climbed to the top of the local water tower, and looked out on the world, literally, on the lights of the town, the flatness, the unrelieved real life that somehow still had to be hopeful. He has never lost that care, or humor, or anger, at what the world wants at times to do to itself. No poet has been more painfully, movingly, *political*—because he has been as all humans only one, yet one of many. He will not yield his specific humanness to God or anyone else.

And last—recalling Ezra Pound's notion, that *only emotion endures*—the range and explicit register of Edward Dorn's ability to *feel* how it actually is to be human, in a given place and time, is phenomenal. So many people will tell you what you're *supposed* to feel, and what a drear bore that is. But in reading these poems, you will hear and feel another human's life as closely and as intimately as that will ever be possible. And that *is* the power of this art.

That said, I can now confess to how intimidating this occasion has been for me. A "preface" for Ed Dorn's poems? Not even a sunrise could quite manage that.

ROBERT CREELEY

Placitas, N.M.
May 28, 1978

SELECTED POEMS

THE RICK OF GREEN WOOD

In the woodyard were green and dry
woods fanning out, behind
                        a valley below
a pleasure for the eye to go.

Woodpile by the buzzsaw. I heard
the woodsman down in the thicket. I don't
want a rick of green wood, I told him
I want cherry or alder or something strong
and thin, or thick if dry, but I don't
want the green wood, my wife would die

Her back is slender
and the wood I get must not
bend her too much through the day.

Aye, the wood is some green
and some dry, the cherry thin of bark
cut in July.

My name is Burlingame
said the woodcutter.
My name is Dorn, I said.
I buzz on Friday if the weather cools
said Burlingame, enough of names.

     Out of the thicket my daughter was walking
singing —
            backtracking the horse hoof
        gone in earlier this morning, the woodcutter's horse
        pulling the alder, the fir, the hemlock
        above the valley
                   in the november

air, in the world, that was getting colder
as we stood there in the woodyard talking
pleasantly, of the green wood and the dry.

[1956]

VAQUERO

The cowboy stands beneath
a brick-orange moon. The top
of his oblong head is blue, the sheath
of his hips
is too.

In the dark brown night
your delicate cowboy stands quite still.
His plain hands are crossed.
His wrists are embossed white.

In the background night is a house,
has a blue chimney top,
Yi Yi, the cowboy's eyes
are blue. The top of the sky
is too.

THE HIDE OF MY MOTHER

1
My mother, who has a hide
on several occasions remarked what

4

a nice rug or robe
my young kids would make,

Would we send them to her?
When we had them butchered?

It was certainly a hoo ha ha
from me
and a ho ho
from my wife: and I would amusedly say
to conceal the fist in my heart
which one? the black?

or the grey
& white?

And she would smile, exposing the carnival
in her head

What's the difference, after they're dead?

Can you imagine asking a poet that?
Perhaps I should tell her about my pet rat.

2
My mother remarked
that in Illinois

little boys sell holly
from door to door,

and *here,* she would say
they grow all over the mountains
what if I took a holly tree back
there? would it grow?
No. I said.

3
Once my mother
was making dinner

and my cats were on the floor.

Why do they whine like that?
she asked,

why don't we throw them all out the door?
why don't you feed them I ventured?

She said she wasn't indentured.

Can you imagine telling a poet that?
Later she fed them my pet rat.

4
One day my son
found a parakeet in the bush
brought it to the house
carrying the little blue thing by the tail.

My mother said why, isn't it pretty,
I wonder if it would make the trip home
to Illinois. Oh, I said, we'll have to find its owner

you don't want to pull a boner
like that.

5
Tho winter's at term
it still gets cold

in the evening.
My pets are warm

because I have set a fire.

My mother is arranging some ferns
and young trees, a little too big

she found in the mountains.
A jig, of a sort must be going

on in her head. It is raining
outside. Do you think I can get the copper legs

of that stool in the box
or is it too wide? With some of those

pretty rocks I saw on the beach, would you,
she was saying to my little boy,

like to go home to Illinois with grandmother?

He was saying from inside the box enclosure,
he wasn't sure he

wanted to leave his mother.

6
For a point of etiquette,
when I observed she was digging
the neighbor's English privet,

I said, it grows in abundance here.

As a matter of fact, she had it,
I thought I saw a rabbit,
that's why I came over here.

I said, a plant like that might grow anywhere.

Well now, I suppose you are right
back home our elms have the blight
but the land is flat there
so many mountains hereabouts

Yes, I allowed, it must help the sprouts . . .

Well now, there's more rain here
than we have in Illinois in an entire year
wouldn't you think tho it would grow there?

I said, what about a privet hedge from . . .

You remember the peonies on grandfather's grave
well someone took them they were gone
the last Memorial Day I was there

. . . From Hudson's Bay to the Gulf of Carpentaria.
Do you think it would stay?

Oh I love plants but where I am the weather
drives the birds away.

7
As for the hides of other people,
My wife told her

of how the junkman's
woman had been so good to us

a truss as it were, had kept the children
when it was a hardship

the condition had been foul, sleet,
masses of air, a raw affair,

dumped out of the Yukon upon
us, roving bands of weather

sliding across British Columbia
a kind of dementia

of the days, frozen water pipes
and the wringer on the washing machine

busted, no coal.
Our house split in two like Pakistan.

The graciousness
of the woman of the junkman

she said. Now what do you think
we should do? forget it? some doughnuts?
a cake?

8

"Why, I don't know what I would do" —
my mother was alluding

to a possible misfortune of her own.

8
As for the thick of it,
really, my mother
never knew about the world.

I mean even that there was one,
or more.

Whorled, like a univalve shell
into herself,

early to bed, nothing
in her head, here and there

Michigan one time,   Ohio

another. Led a life
like a novel, who hasn't?

As for Sociology:
garbage cans were what she dumped
the remains of supper in,

dirty newspapers, if blowing
in the street, somebody probably

dropped them there.

Nobody told her about the damned
or martyrdom. She's 47

so that, at least, isn't an emergency.

Had a chance to go to Arizona once
and weighed the ins and outs

to the nearest ounce:
didn't go. She was always slow.

Incidently, for her the air
was Red one time:

tail end of a dust storm
somehow battered up from Kansas.

ARE THEY DANCING

There is a sad carnival up the valley
The willows flow it seems on trellises of music
Everyone is there today, everyone I love.

There is a mad mad fiesta along the river
Thrilling ladies sing in my ear, where
Are your friends, lost? They were to come

And banjoes were to accompany us all
And our feet were to go continually
The sound of laughter was to flow over the water

What was to have been, is something else
I am afraid. Only a letter from New Mexico
And another from a mountain by Pocatello,

I wonder, what instruments are playing
And whose eyes are straying over the mountain
Over the desert
And are they dancing: or gazing at the earth.

GERANIUM

I know that peace is soon coming, and love of common object,
and of woman and all the natural things I groom, in my mind, of
faint rememberable patterns, the great geography of my lunacy.

I go on my way frowning at novelty, wishing I were closer to home
than I am. And this is the last bus stop before Burlington,
that pea-center, which is my home, but not the home of my mind.
That asylum I carry in my insane squint, where beyond
the window a curious woman in the station door
has a red bandana on her head, and tinkling things hand themselves
to the wind that gathers about her skirts. In the rich manner of her kind
she waits for the bus to stop. Lo, a handsome woman.

Now, my sense decays, she is the flat regularity, the brick
of the station wall, is the red Geranium of my last Washington stop.
Is my object no shoes brought from india
can make exotic, nor hardly be made antic would she astride
a motorcycle (forsake materials and we shall survive together)
nor be purchased by the lust of schedule.

No,

on her feet therefore, are the silences of nothing. And leather
leggings adorn her limbs, on her arms are the garlands of ferns
come from a raining raining forest and dripping lapidary's dust.
She is a common thief of fauna and locale (in her eyes
are the small sticks of slender land-bridges) a porter
standing near would carry her bundle, which is scarlet too,

as a geranium and cherishable common that I worship and that I sing
ploddingly, and out of tune as she, were she less the lapwing
as she my pale sojourner, is.

THE AIR OF JUNE SINGS

Quietly and while at rest on the trim grass I have gazed,
admonished myself for having never been here
at the grave-side and read the names of my Time Wanderers.
And now, the light noise of the children at play on the inscribed stone

jars my ear and they whisper and laugh covering their mouths. "My
    Darling"
my daughter reads, some of the markers
reflect such lightness to her reading eyes, yea, as I rove
among these polished and lime blocks I am moved to tears and I hear
the depth in "Darling, we love thee," and as in "Safe in Heaven."

I am going off to heaven and I won't see you anymore. I am
going back into the country and I won't be here anymore. I am
going to die in 1937. But where did you die my Wanderer?
You, under the grave-grass, with the tin standard whereat
I look, and try to read the blurred ink. I cannot believe
you were slighted knowing what I do of cost and evil
yet tin is less than granite. Those who buried you should have known
a 6 inch square of sandstone, flush with the earth
is more proper for the gone than blurred and faded flags.

Than the blurred and faded flags I am walking with in the graveyard.

Across the road in the strawberry field two children are stealing
their supper fruit, abreast in the rows, in the fields of the overlord,
Miller his authentic name, and I see that name represented here,
there is that social side of burial too, long residence,
and the weight of the established local dead. My eyes avoid
the largest stone, larger than the common large, Goodpole Matthews,
Pioneer, and that pioneer sticks in me like a wormed black cherry
in my throat, No Date, nothing but that zeal, that trekking
and Business, that presumption in a sacred place, where children
are buried, and where peace, as it is in the fields and the country
should reign. A wagon wheel is buried there. Lead me away

to the small quiet stones of the unpreposterous dead and leave
me my tears for Darling we love thee, for Budded on earth and
    blossomed
in heaven, where the fieldbirds sing in the fence rows,
and there is possibility, where there are not the loneliest of all.

Oh, the stones not yet cut.

SOUSA

Great brass bell of austerity
and the ghosts of old picnickers
ambling under the box elder, when the sobriety
was the drunkenness. John,

you child, there is no silence
you can't decapitate
and on forgotten places (the octagonal
stand, Windsor, Illinois, the only May Day
of my mind) the fresh breeze
and the summer dresses of girls once blew
but do not now. They blow now at the backs
of our ears John,
under the piñon,
that foreign plant with arrogant southern smell.
I yearn for the box elder and its beautiful
bug, the red striped and black plated—
your specific insect, in the Sunday after noon.

Oh restore my northern madness
which no one values anymore and shun
its uses, give them back their darkened instinct
(which I value no more) we are
dedicated to madness that's why I love you
Sousa, you semper fidelis maniac.

And the sweep
of your american arms
bring a single banging street in Nebraska
home, and your shock
when a trillion broads smile at you
their shocking laughter can be heard long after
the picknickers have gone home.

March us home through the spring rain
the belief, the relief
of sunday occasion.

Your soft high flute and brass
remind me of a lost celebration I can't
quite remember,
in which I volunteered as conqueror:
the silence now stretches me
into sadness.

Come back into the street bells
and tin soldiers.

•   •

But there are no drums
no drums, loudness,
no poinsettia shirts,
there is no warning, you won't recognize anyone.

Children and men in every way
milling, gathering daily (those vacant eyes)
the bread lines of the deprived are here
Los Alamos, 1960, not Salinas
not Stockton.

Thus when mouths are opened,
waves of poison rain will fall, butterflies
do not fly up from any mouth in this place.

      •   •

Let me go away,
shouting alone, laughing
to the air, Sousa be here
when the leaves wear
a blank radio green, for honoring.

    Dwell again in the hinterland
and take your phone,
play to the lovely eyed people in the field
on the hillside.

Hopeful, and kind
merrily and possible
(as my friend said, "Why can't it be
like this all the time?"
her arms spread out before her).

      •   •

John Sousa you can't now
amuse a nation with colored drums
even with cymbals, their ears
have lifted the chalice of explosion
a glass of straight malice, and
we wander in Random in the alleys
of their longfaced towns taking
from their sickly mandibles handbills
summoning our joint spirits.

I sing Sousa.

The desire to disintegrate the Earth
is eccentric,
And away from centre
nothing more nor sizeable
nor science

nor ennobling
no purity, no endeavor
toward human grace.

• •

We were
on a prominence though
so lovely to the eye eyes
of birds only caught
all the differences
of each house filled hill.

And from the window a spire
of poplar, windows
and brown pater earth buildings.

My eye on the circling bird
my mind lost in the rainy hemlocks of Washington
the body displaced, let it
wander all the way to Random and dwell
in those damp groves
where stand the friends
I love and left: behind me
slumbering under the dark morning sky

are my few friends.

Please
cut wood to warm them
and stalk never appearing animals
to warm them,
I hope they are warm tonight—
bring salmonberries
even pumpkinseed.

Sousa,
it can never be
as my friend said
"Why can't it be like this all the time?"
Her arms spread out before her

gauging the alarm,
(with that entablature)
and the triumph of a march
in which no one
is injured.

A COUNTRY SONG

> *"And I pluck'd a hollow reed,*
> *And I made a rural pen"*
>
> BLAKE

1
Thru the window
Cherry tree limbs

Thru the country
The air climbs

Over the fields
And along the road

The country woman
Comes to her abode

Over a letter
Her eye wanders

From a sister
Who wonders

How she is there
On the farm

In the country air.

2
Thru the window
The cherry branch

Against the bright sky
I in this room chance

To set my head
Against the wall

Awaiting the woman
Her entering footfall

On the porch, saying—
Sit down

And stay awhile
Here's a letter from town

And did you see
The daffodils

Spring, is coming early.

3
Thru the window
The cherry broods

—We've come here, sat
We haven't stood

Nor waited long
The quiet is amazing

And the stove fire
Very blazing

It must be wild
To get drunk on the country

In the cold burning air
When the orchard is empty

When winter stares with sloe eye
Thru bright windows

And Spring, is coming early.

4
Thru the window
The man stood

Against a rake
He broods

By a burning bush
He thinks of the ground

And the garden
To be grown

And the harvest
To be gathered

In the fall.
A winter-time piece tethered

In his eye
Ideas of the land

Under a cold blue sky.

5
Thru the windows
The man's hair

Shines white his bright
Bush dies in the fair

Wind, and he throws
The remaining sticks

On the fire then looks
Toward the house and picks

Up the tools
The children run

To greet him, they enter
The house with the sun

Going down under the tree
What a wild thing

To be in the country.

6
Thru the door
They come

Thru the day
They have gone

As the world turned
Around

He cleared the
Beckoning ground

Now the yellow strings
Of dusk hang in the air

They read the letter
From the sister,

Then in front of the fire
We talk of Spring

An obscure slight offering.

PRAYERS FOR THE PEOPLE OF THE WORLD

They were an exercise the ages go through
smiling in the church one time
banging and blowing in the street another
where brother is a state very often of glue
coming apart in the heat
of British Guiana where
the drainage and open canals
make difficult the protection of the lower classes
who have lands and moneys, food and shelter
in the great escrow called Never

Did America say give me your poor?
Yes for poor is the vitamin not stored
it goes out in the urine of all endeavor.
So Poor came in long black flea coats
and bulgarian hats
spies and bombers
and she made five rich while flies covered the rest
who were suppressed or murdered
or out-bred their own demise.

THERE WAS A CHANGE

the weather broke up
like rocks, landslides
in the sky's terrain
all falling down
to where a palisade of white
now holds the horizon.

On the mountains
which are an appellation
of blood called sangre
                the white spears
of slopes cut down
into the lower altitudes

a firm thrust, a decision
at this height,
and for those things.

                The apricot
is the first to bloom
then comes the apple.
Already the blossom
                of the apricot
has gone,
                the clouds
are drifting up on the breeze
their darkening undersides
                        the ballast
of a change.

And all our friends will return
crossing the dry frontier river
traveling north.

HI   a change in the weather.
HI   a friend's return.

IF IT SHOULD EVER COME

And we are all there together
time will wave as willows do
and adios will be truly, yes,

    laughing at what is forgotten
and talking of what's new
admiring the roses you brought.
How sad.

You didn't know you were at the end
thought it was your bright pear
the earth, yes

another affair to have been kept
and gazed back on
when you had slept
to have been stored
as a squirrel will a nut, and half
forgotten,
there were so many, many
from the newly fallen.

HOME ON THE RANGE, FEBRUARY, 1962

Flutes, and the harp on the plain
Is a distance, of pain, and waving reeds
The scale of far off trees, notes not of course
Upon a real harp but chords in the thick clouds
And the wind reaching its arms toward west yellowstone.
Moving to the east, the grass was high once, and before
White wagons moved

                the hawk, proctor of the hills still is

Oh god did the chunky westerner think to remake this in his own
    image
Oh god did the pioneer society sanctify the responsible citizen
To do that
            face like a plot of ground
Was it iron locomotives and shovels, hand tools
And barbed wire motives for each man's
Fenced off little promised land

                        or the mind of bent

Or of carson, oh earp
These sherpas of responsible destruction
Posses led by a promising girl wielding a baton upon the street
A Sacagawea wearing a baseball cap, eating a Clark bar.
And flutes and the harp are on the plain
Bring the last leading edge of stillness
Brought no water, brought dead roots
Like an allotment of tool handles to their premises—and they cry
In pain over daily income—a hundred years of planned greed
Loving the welfare state of new barns and bean drills
Hot passion for the freedom of the dentist!
Their plots were america's first subdivisions called homesteads

Lean american—gothic quarter sections gaunt look
Managing to send their empty headed son who is a ninny
to nebraska to do it, all over again, to the ground, a prairie
Dog hole,
And always they smirk at starvation
And consider it dirty . . . a joke their daughters learn
From their new husbands.

ON THE DEBT MY MOTHER OWED TO SEARS ROEBUCK

Summer was dry, dry the garden
our beating hearts, on that farm, dry
with the rows of corn the grasshoppers
came happily to strip, in hordes, the first
thing I knew about locust was they came
dry under the foot like the breaking of
a mechanical bare heart which collapses
from an unkind an incessant word whispered
in the house of the major farmer
and the catalogue company,
from no fault of anyone
my father coming home tired
and grinning down the road, turning in
is the tank full? thinking of the horse
and my lazy arms thinking of the water
so far below the well platform.

On the debt my mother owed to sears roebuck
we brooded, she in the house, a little heavy
from too much corn meal, she
a little melancholy from the dust of the fields
in her eye, the only title she ever had to lands—
and man's ways winged their way to her through the mail
saying so much per month
so many months, this is yours, take it
take it, take it, take it
and in the corncrib, like her lives in that house
the mouse nibbled away at the cob's yellow grain
until six o'clock when her sorrows grew less
and my father came home

On the debt my mother owed to sears roebuck?
I have nothing to say, it gave me clothes to
wear to school,
and my mother brooded

in the rooms of the house, the kitchen, waiting
for the men she knew, her husband, her son
from work, from school, from the air of locusts
and dust masking the hedges of fields she knew
in her eye as a vague land where she lived,
boundaries, whose tractors chugged pulling harrows
pulling discs, pulling great yields from the earth
pulse for the armies in two hemispheres, 1943
and she was part of that *stay at home army* to keep
things going, owing that debt.

WAGON WHEELS

Hands on a surcingle
hands on a hackamore
demanding because they paid
their money
to be like the first blackamoor
    in these parts
strange cowboys live
in ranch style houses.

Say one of them sees
his horse every day or so
like that,
but another wants the west wide
like that, refusing
population, a monster to him.

Yet exhausted it still moves
across "the precious uncluttered
land" as its will takes it
plastic boats behind.

LOS MINEROS

Now it is winter and the fallen snow
has made its stand on the mountains, making dunes
of white on the hills, drifting over
the flat valley floors, and the cold cover
has got us out to look for fuel.

First to Madrid which is 4 miles beyond Cerillos
close to the Golden Mountains
a place whose business once throve like the clamor in Heorot Hall;
but this was not sporting business, The Mine Explosion of 1911.
And on the wall in the mine office

                                 there in Madrid

are two pictures of those blackbirds, but a time later;
the thirties, and the bite of the depression is no bleaker
on their faces than is the coming morning of the day they were
       took.
These men whom we will never know are ranged 14 in number
in one of those pictures that are very long, you've seen them.

And the wonder is five are smiling Mexicanos, the rest
could be English or German, blown to New Mexico on another
winter's snow. Hard to imagine Spanish as miners, their
sense is good-naturedly above ground (and their cruelty).
In a silly way they know their pictures are being taken,

and know it isn't necessary honor standing in line with their hands
       hiding
in their pockets. I was looking to see if they are short
as Orwell says miners must be, but they aren't save two
little Mexican boys. What caught my eye at first was the way
they were so finely dressed in old double-breasted suit coats, ready
      for work.

Then I looked into their faces and the races separated.
The English or Germans wear a look which is mystic in its
      expectancy;

able men underground,
but the Spanish face carries no emergency
and one of the little boys, standing behind a post
looks right out of the picture faintly smiling: even today. Martine
whom I had gone with was waiting for the weight slip.
When we got over to the giant black chute the man above waved
as from the deck of a troubled ship and said no carbon
amigos, and then climbed down the ladder.

Madrid is a gaunt town now. Its houses stand unused
along the entering road, and they are all green and white,
every window has been abused with the rocks of departing childr

IN MY YOUTH I WAS A TIRELESS DANCER

But now I pass
graveyards in a car.
The dead lie,
unsuperstitiously,
with their feet toward me—
please forgive me for
saying the tombstones would not
fancy their faces turned from the highway.

Oh perish the thought
I was thinking in that moment
Newman Illinois
the Saturday night dance—
what a life!   Would I like it again?
No.   Once I returned late summer
from California thin from journeying
and the girls were not the same.
You'll say that's natural
they had been dancing all the time.

FROM GLOUCESTER OUT

It has all
come back today.
That memory for me is nothing
there ever was,
            That man

so long,
when stretched out
and so bold
            on his ground
and so much
lonely anywhere.

But never to forget
                  that moment

when we came out of the tavern
and wandered through the carnival.
They were playing
the washington post march
but I mistook it for manhattan beach
for all around were the colored lights
of delirium
            to the left the boats
of Italians
and ahead of us, past the shoulders
of St. Peter the magician of those fishermen

the bay
stood, and immediately in it the silent
inclined pole where tomorrow the young men
of this colony
so dangerous on the street
will fall harmlessly
into the water.

They are not the solid
but are the solidly built
citizens, and they are about us
as we walk across
                    the square
with their black provocative
women
slender, like whips of
sex in the sousa filled night.

Where edged
by that man in the music
of a transplanted time and
enough of drunkenness
to make you senseless of all
but virtue
                    (there is never
no, there is never a small complaint)
(that all things shit poverty,
and Life, one wars on with
many embraces) oh it was a time that was perfect
but for my own hesitating
to know all I had not known.
Pure existence, even in the crowds
I love
will never be possible for me

even with the men I love
                    This is
the guilt
that kills me
            My adulterated presence

but please believe with all men
I love to be
•

That memory
of how he lay out

30

on the floor in his great length
and when morning came,
late,
we lingered
in the vastest of all cities
in this hemisphere
                    and all other movement
stopped, nowhere
else was there a stirring known to us

yet that morning I stood
by the window up 3 levels
and watched a game
of stick ball, thinking of going away,
and wondering what would befall that man
when he returned to his territory.
The street as you could guess
was thick with their running
and cars,
themselves, paid that activity
such respect I thought a ritual
in the truest sense,
where all time and all motion
part around the space of men
in that act
as does a river flow past
the large rock.

•

And he slept.
in the next room, waiting
in an outward slumber
                    for the time

we climbed into the car, accepting all things
from love, the currency of which is
parting, and glancing.

Then went
out of that city to jersey .

where instantly we could not find our way
and the maze of the outlands west
starts that quick
where you may touch
your finger to liberty
and look so short a space
to the columnar bust
of New York
and know those people exist
as a speck in your own lonely heart
who will shortly depart,
taking a conveyance for the
radial stretches
past girls on corners
past drugstores, tired hesitant
creatures who I also love
in all their alienation were it not so
past all equipment of country side
to temporary homes
where the wash of sea and other
populations come
once more to whisper only one thing
for all people: a late and far-away
night yearning for
and when he gets there
I want him to stay away
from the taverns of familiarity
I want him to walk by the seashore alone
in all height
which is nothing more than
a mountain. Or the hailing of a mast
with big bright eyes.

So rushing,
          all the senses
come to him
as a swarm of golden bees
and their sting is the power
he uses as parts of

the oldest brain. He hears
the delicate thrush
of the water attacking
He hears the cries, falling gulls
and watches silently the gesture of grey
bygone people. He hears their cries
and messages, he never

ignores any sound.
As they come to him he places them
puts clothes upon them
and gives them their place
in their new explanation, there is never
a lost time, nor any inhabitant
of that time to go split by prisms or unplaced
and unattended,
               that you may believe

is the breath he gives
the great already occurred and nightly beginning world.
So with the populace of his mind
you think his nights? are not
lonely. My God. Of his
loves, you know nothing and of his
false beginning
you can know nothing,
                but this thing to be marked
again

    only

he who worships the gods with his strictness
can be of their company
the cat and the animals, the bird he took
from the radiator
of my car saying it had died
a natural death, rarely seen in a bird.

To play, as areal particulars can out of the span
of Man, and of all, this man

does not
        he, does, he
    walks
            by the sea
in my memory

and sees all things and to him
are presented at night
the whispers of the most flung shores
from Gloucester out

                    [1964]

IDAHO OUT

For Hettie and Roi

> *"The thing to be known is the natural
> landscape. It becomes known through
> the totality of its forms."*– CARL O. SAUER

1
Since 1925 there are now no
negative areas he has ignored
the poles have been strung for our time together
and his hand is in the air as well

areal is hopefully Ariel

        So black & red simplot fertilizer smoke

drifts its excremental way
down the bottle of our
valley
toward the narrowing
end

coming into the portneuf gap
where its base aspects . . .
a large cork could be placed
but which proceeding from inkom

                              or toward

past the low rooves
of sheep's sheds the slope
gains rough brusque edges
and you are in it more quickly
than its known forms allow

        or the approach from
the contrary side of the valley
there is a total journal
with the eyes
and the full gap stands
as the grand gate from our
place
to utah bad lands and
thus down
to those sullen valleys
of men who have apparently
accepted all of the vital
factor of their time
not including humanity.

    And not to go too far with them
they were the first white flour makers

            they jealously
keep that form and turn the sides

of the citizens' hills into square documents
of their timid endeavor. The only
hard thing they had was first massacre
and then brickwork
not propaedeutic to a life of grand design
wherein *all* men fit

                              but something
for all its pleasure of built surface
and logic of substances as
the appeal of habitat
     for salt lake downtown is
     not ugly,
     but to a life of petty retreat
     before such small concourses
     as smoking, drinking, and other less
     obvious but
     justly necessary bodily needs
     not including breeding which in their hands
     is purposive.

From this valley
there is no leaving by laterals.
Even george goodhart,
a conventional man, as all
good hearts are
knew, with a horse
and access crosswise
to creekheads
the starving indian women could be fed
with surplus deer.

Who was the pioneer boy who died in a rest home
and was a new local, i.e.,
there is implied evidence
he never heard the cry of the pawnee
in his territory.
Which, it is said in the human
ecology term
is to be a hick, howsoever travelled. And
while we are at it it is best said here:
The mark of the pre-communication
westerner

travelled in local segments
along a line of time
utterly sequestered
thus his stupidity required the services
of at least one of his saddle bags
and, in the meantime
his indian friends
signalled one another over his head
as he passed on his businesslike way
in the depressions
between them, in long shadows
they looking deaf and dumb, moving fingers
on the slight rounds
of nebraskan hills.

Of a verge

of the land North
and an afternoon is no good
there is the width of the funnel rim
and sad people for all their smiles
do scurry and sing across its mouth
and there are no archipelagoes of real laughter

in alameda
and no really wild people save stiff
inhibited criminals.

So when gay youth was yours
in those other smaller towns on the peneplain
of central america and the jerseys
the white legs of girls stand truly by stoplights
and Edward Hopper truly did stop painting
all those years. But we stray
we strays, as we always do
and those mercies always wanted

an endless price, our jazz came

from the same hip shops we walked past
the truly, is no sense speaking of universes,
hanging from that hook

I had in mind the sweet shop
something so simple as main street
and I'll be around.

But I was escorting you out of Pocatello,
sort of north.
Perhaps past that physiographic
menace the arco desert and
what's there
of the leakage of newclear seance

to Lemhi
again a mormon nomenclature
where plaques to the journey of Lewis & Clark
but the rises across the too
tilted floors of that corridor
at high point the birch
and then toward North Fork
you must take that
other drainage where yes
the opposites are so sheer
and the fineness of what growth
there is that lifting
following
of line, the forever bush
and its thin colored sentinelling
of those streams
as North Fork comes on
on the banks of the magnificent salmon
we come smack up on a marvelous beauty from Chi.

Who has
a creaky cheap pooltable
to pass the winter with
and the innocent loudmouthed handsome
boys who inhabit the

winter there. The remarkably quiet winter
there,
all alone where the salmon forks.
It is so far away but never long ago.
You may be sure Hudson.
And
She said
shaking her dark hair
she used to work at arco
and knew the fastest way
from salmon to idaho falls—
you may be sure
and in a car

        or anywhere,

she was a walking invitation
to a lovely party
her body was that tactile to the eye
or what I meant
she is part
of the morphology
the last distant place of idaho north,
already in effect Montana.
Thus, roughly free,
to bring in relative terms.
Her husband, though it
makes no difference,
had sideburns, wore
a kind of abstract spats
wore loose modern beltless pants
and moved with that accord to the earth
I deal with
but only the heavy people
are with.
   They are "the pragmatic 'and'
the always unequated remnant"

2
My desire is to be
a classical poet
my gods have been men . . .
and women.
I renew my demand
that presidents and chairmen everywhere
be moved to a quarantine outside the earth
somewhere,
as we travel northward. My
peculiar route is across
the lost trail pass past
in the dark draws somewhere
my north fork beauty's husband's
dammed up small dribbling creek

fetching a promising lake (she showed
me the pictures) a too good to be true
scheme she explained to me,
to draw fishermen with hats on
from everywhere
they wanted to come from.
One of the few ventures I've
given my blessing . . . she
would look nice rich.

3
We were hauling . . .
furniture. To Missoula.
We stopped in the biting
star lit air often to have
a beer and stretch our legs.

My son rode with me
and was delighted that a state
so civilized as Montana
could exist, where the people,
and no matter how small

the town,
and how disconnected in
the mountain trails,
could be so welcoming to a lad,
far from the prescribed ages
of idaho where they chase that
young population out, into
the frosty air. There is
an incredible but true fear
of the trespassing there of such
patently harmless people aged 13.

But not to go too much into
that ethnic shit, because
this is geographic business
already, in the bitteroot
there sat snow on the tallest
peaks and that moisture factor
caused trees now gliding by
from one minor drainage
to another until we came
to the great bitterroot
proper and the cottonwoods
and feather honey locusts
lining its rushing edges.
Once, when I was going the other way
in august,
a lemhi rancher
told me the soil content
of the bitterroot was of
such a makeup that the cows
got skinnier whereas
in the lemhi, you know
the rest, although of course
the lemhi is dry. It's
like a boring popular song
all by himself he'd love
to rest his weary head
on somebody else's shoulder
as he grows older.

From Florence to Missoula
is a very pragmatic distance
And florence is the singularity
Montana has, one is so drunk
by that time. Fort Benton,
to your right, across stretches
of the cuts of the Blackfoot, through
Bowman's Corner, no
the sky

is not

bigger in Montana. When
for instance you come
from Williston
there seems at the border a change
but it is only because man has
built a tavern there
and proclaims himself of service
at a point in time, very much,
and space is continuous from Superior
to Kalispell. And indeed

That is what the dirtiest
of human proportions are built on
service by men there before you

could have possibly come
and you never can.

But if men can live in Moab
that itself is proof nature
is on the run and seeding very badly
and that environmentalism, old word,
is truly dead.

4
So he goes anywhere apparently
anywhere and space is muddied
with his tracks

42

for ore he is only after,
after ore.
He is the most regretful factor
in a too minuscule cosmic
the universe it turns out your neighbors are

The least obnoxious of all
the radiating circles bring
grossnesses
that are of the strength of bad dreams.

5
Let me remind you we were in Florence
Montana.
Where the Bitterroot is thick
past Hamilton, a farm machinery
nexus
for all that unnutritious hay
and in florence we stop.

Everyone gets out of the trucks
and stretching & yawning moves
through the biting still starlit night
a night covered with jewels
and the trucks' radiators begin
to creak and snap in their cooling off.

We shiver. Each limbjoint
creaks and shudders and we talk
in chatters of the past road, of the failing
head lights on the mountain road—and in
we go.

        A wildly built girl
brushes past us
as we enter. Inside
it is light, a funny disinherited place
of concrete block. The fat woman
bartender,

has an easy smile as we head for the fireplace
in the rear and as we go by the box is putting out
some rock and twist, and on the table
by the fireplace there are canned things, string beans
and corn, and she brings us the beer.

Florence. It is hardly a place.
To twist it, it is a wide spot
in the valley. The air is cold. The fire
burns into our backs while we sit on the hearth.
The girl of the not quite
believable frame
returns, and her boyfriend is pulled
by the vertically rhythmic tips of her fingers
reluctantly off the stool,
but he can't
he, the conservative under riding buttress
of our planet can't, he has been drinking beer
while she, too young for a public place
has been pulling a bottle apart in the car.

So there you are. She is
as ripe and bursting as that
biblical pomegranate.
She bleeds spore in her
undetachable black pants
and, not to make it seem too good
or even too remote
or too unlikely near
she has that
kind of generous smile
offset by a daring and hostile look
again, I must insist, her hair
was black, the color of hostile sex
the lightest people, for all
their odd beauty,
are a losing game.

. . . I can't leave her.
Her mother was with her.

She, in the tavern, in Florence
was ready,
with all her jukeboxbody
and her trips to the car
to the bottle.
There are many starry nights thus occupied
while the planet, indifferent, rattles on
like the boxcars on its skin
and when moments like that transpire
they with all good hope begin again somewhere
She made many trips to the car that night . . .
an unmatchable showoff
with her eyes
and other accomplishments.

6
And onward
bless us, there are no eyes
in Missoula, only things, the new
bridge across Clark Fork
there is civilization again,
a mahogany bar
                    and tickertape

baseball, and the men are men,
but there are no eyes
in Missoula
like in little orphan annie and is?
the sky bigger there?

        The sky disdains
to be thus associated and treacherous cowboys
who drive cars live there.
Say the purity of blue over Houston
that unwholesome place
is prettier
and the graininess over Michoacan is moodier
and I have been to wyoming.

7

The trip back sadly as all trips
back are
        dull
and I did
see the old bartender woman of florence
this time in her restaurant part 50 yards
away from the tavern between which
she ran apparently with the speed
of some sort of stout gazelle
but not the broad with the fabulatory build.
She that day was probably off in an office somewhere.
Pity daytime lives.

But everyone was tired. We had unloaded
the furniture, early the next morning
and before the bite of the sun quelled the bite
of the stars we left, going the long, time consuming
way
south. Sober business.
The Beauty of North Fork was there as she will be
till she dies sometime
(and by the way she runs a tavern)
Thence to salmon and across the narrow bridge
and out
into the lemhi. I say
if it weren't for the distances
and for the trees & creeks I would
go mad, o yes, land, that one forces
a secondary interest in, vanishes
as a force as you drive onward.
This is only obvious.
This is only some of the times we spend.
You go through it as though it were
a planet of cotton wadding . . . and love
its parts as you do the parts of a woman
whose relations with earth are more established
than your own.

But of physical entirety
there is no need to elaborate, one has
one's foot
on the ground, which is the saying
of all common and communicable pleasures
and my arm around your shoulder is the proof of that.
But I am ashamed of my country
that, not as areal reality, but as act
it shames me to be a citizen in
the land where I grew up. The very air chills
your bones, the very ungraciousness of its replies
and the pressures of its not replying
embarrass my presence here. God knows
we do what we can to live.
But the intimidations thrown at us
in the spurious forms they have learned truth
can take, in a time which should have been
plenty and engaging of the best that each man,
if he were encouraged to be even that, and
not slapped in the face as stupid, cut off
from all other peoples to make him hygienic of
views not viable to this soil, which is no more
sacred I tell you than any other the earth
has to offer, for she in her roundness has kept
an accord with her movements great time has not yet
seen aberrant. Mice crawling on a moving body?
can they, may they really offset great movement?

The very air,
if you are awake, can chill your bones
and there is little enough of beauty
finally scratched for. It is not
the end pursuit of my countrymen
that they be great
in a great line of men.
An occasional woman, won't,
though I wish she could,
justify a continent. In the parliaments
of minuscule places she is there

and gives them substance,
as in Florence, and North Fork
for she was gracious as leaders
are now not and I begin to believe after all
these years there *is* an aristocracy
of place and event and person
and as I sit here above this valley
I sought to involve you with
and take you out on a trip
that had no point, there remains Montana
          and it is nice. But not infallible.
The sky is a hoax.
And was meant,
once suggested,
to catch your eye. The eye
can be arbitrary,
but its subject matter cannot.
Thus the beauty of some women.
And from Williston
along the grand missourian length
of the upper plains you go, then the Milk
to Havre
that incredible distance once along a route
all those clamorous men
took . . . they now grow things there not horticultural
only storageable, things of less importance
than fur
for furs then were never stockpiled, it would
hurt the hair,
                    that Astor,
he'd never have done it.

And yes Fort Benton is lovely
and quiet, I would gladly give it as a gift
to a friend, and with pride, a place of marked
indolence, where the river closes, a gift
of marked indifference, if it were mine.
If the broad grass park were mine
between the river and the town

and to the quick rise behind.
And then up to the median altitude of Montana
Sugar beets and sheep and cattle.

Where the normal spaces
are the stretches of Wyoming
and north Dakota, Idaho
is cut
by an elbow
of mountain that swings
down, thus she is
cut off by geologies she says
I'm sure
are natural
but it is truly the West
as no other place,
ruined by an ambition and religion
cut, by a cowboy use of her nearly virgin self

       unannealed
by a real placement
               this,

this
is the birthplace
of Mr. Pound
and Hemingway in his own mouth
chose to put a shotgun.

SIX VIEWS FROM THE SAME WINDOW
OF THE NORTHSIDE GROCERY

(for Helene on Washington's birthday)

1

Saturday afternoon. The hill is a reminder
with its slope of a counterpart outside
Sedro Woolley—wooded second growth there
snow and the black scars of juniper here.
The glass shines with the land beyond
red freight cars and the vast house of shops.

2

We occupy red enameled chairs
in the backroom, drink beer and eat greek
cheese and olives, white salt of the cheese
black salt of the shrivelled olive spit
into the ash tray. Beyond the old pink front
the red green stripes of the awning sway in the breeze
of these last days of February. All the panes
remarkable of clarity, an uncle sam kite
writhes up from the hands of the black boy
the rattle of its paper cannot be heard.

3

Goat cheese and greek olives. The owner
is sullen and friendly, he calls the black women sister
they come and go inside his grocery, one thing at a time
it does not pretend to be a small supermarket.
Cold air, clean glass. We rest and watch.
The occasion for this excursion is in the selected strings
of a life gone terribly lonely. It will be a march.
A frail cloud moves with silence into the window.
No sound in the store. No bell on the door.

4

The dark children fly their kite—
we share a common exile—they run
I stay here in the woven light
of a backroom.
It is pointless to make verse of this fibre. I could write
all the names of my absent friends
on the window in black
and the light would grow less
and then lesser
and I would sit motionless
on the dark side of my thought
I would sit in the deep shade of my yearning
I would have supplied me the proper nouns
of my darkness.

5

And my lady looks from the same window, over
one yard altogether away, another picture
of the world, white house isolated, a lost railroad
building, this vast change rung with the same air
and we are, by the same air, a rest of those
measures of wood, of the same kite, cans bounded
by trash she has in her view, and poles
of loosely hung wire, some power lost altogether
back of the glass as the trembling portrait
of uncle sam, of all the continuing weirdness
in the ennui of the falling sun, and I stare at her
and her lips part very little, slow and pleasantly
vagrant talk, the measures are the stillnesses
made various by the code of friends' names, those nouns
drop like greek olives from our fingers, and the pits
are in a real way the crashing verbs of
a mistaken local rapport. Be patient
and give me your hand, there is something of a beginning
everywhere, this is a new part of town.

6

There is a part of the world over your shoulder
can't be seen in a window and can't be pulled
through the holes in one's eyes yet a fixture
of some boundaries is a small cure haphazardly grasped
or torn loose from a confused day, a tiresomeness
arrived with a permanent smile hand outstretched
I love you now more than ever and stand waving my arms
at the edge of a swarm of self breeding considerations
to say it, the mailbox, that post, is sought out
by both of us a triangulation of what we share
as elsewhere,
it is a twin exile, the small town's portion
of futility, the self mockery with an interchangeable tire
that makes us dare what we are. Thus a window
is that seemingly clear opening our tested knowledges
pass through and the world shakes not at all
before the weight of our appointments, you will
and would be part of the new hemisphere
until it dies of the same old loosely wrought manifestoes.
All those sounds from the broken washing machine
are trying to tell you something sweetheart don't laugh
one day it will speak and not stop
all things have an insistence of their own.

SONG

Christ of the sparrows Help me!
  the soot falls
    along the street
  into the alleys.
december.

and sometimes
  its rain falls
    along pocatello's streets
  into its alleys
  along its black diesel thruways

There is no far away place
could satisfy
there is no forlorn bird
could outdistance my desire.
When the vacation
of my heart is that complete
the pain of this
particular moment
is unbearable. The sun
strikes my book laden table
my room is my skull
I could have you tell me
this pain behind my eyes will soon be gone
I could listen, I could die
seized by a foolishly contrived misunderstanding

or listlessly watch
    the two single
figures bent
and in the rags of careful hesitation
feel their way along the sidewalk
past my window
old men

leave a city already made lonely
by the outcast words of pointless conversation
  go,
along the intolerably windy highway west of here.

  And mind us
there were no marks of the bruise of friends
there aren't any traces of that turmoil, you stay
as you were, there were
a few headlong pitches onto the ground
a torn shoulder to remember
a few unhappy nights.
drunk with the high necessity to talk
fast and loud in crowded bars
And then, in the street
to spit silently out
the cheap guilt
and all the casual half meant and self aware
inward chastisement
a petty reward for myself, like saving a nickel
and insisting even with a smile
it was *my* life I lived
the suspicious terror I'd turned around
too many times to keep track
I said you said I said You said I said.

THE SMUG NEVER SILENT GUNS OF THE ENEMY

Their muzzles are at the door.
Did you see them, did he
see them, minutemen
rising out of the silos
A winter wonderland of
the white busy north.
The smug guns, trained on
The whites of their eyes
are grey
        and disputations
of more guns come
into the ear:
    The manipulated price of sugar
    The death of great ladies
    "I'll shoot my second if you'll shoot yours"
    Concentrated insecticides
    (flow like milk in the river
    You will be greeted
    on the outskirts of town
    with a vegetable brush
    and tips on good living

    An interview with a turkey farmer
        (gobbling in the background
the news that Bertrand Russell
    is a sick old fool
    The seminar ends when the squat madeyed colonel
    announces the way to peace thru war and shoots the moderator

And more corrupted reports follow you out
the door, they implore you to think young
and you do
it is such a pleasure in the sagebrush
in the open saturated air
zipping up your pants
having made more of the latest news
on the new snow.

SONG: VENCEREMOS

(for latin america
(for préman sotomayor

And there will be fresh children once more
in planalto and matto grosso
green mansions for their houses
along the orinoco
  take away the oil
  it is not to anoint their heads
  take away the cannon
  and the saber from the paunch belly
  overlaid with crossed colors
  those quaint waddling men
  are the leaden dead toys
         only their

      own

      children

        caress
  while the great eyed children
  far away in the mountains, out of Quito
  pass thru the crisp evening streets
  of earth towns, where they caress
  the earth, a substance of *majority*
  including the lead of established
  forces,
who can do nothing
  but give us the measures of pain
    which now define us

Take away the boats from the bananas
they are there for the double purpose
to quell insurrection first

and next to make of an equatorial food
a clanging and numerical register in chicago
this is not an industrial comment,
it is not Sandburg's chicago
not how ugly a city you did make
but whitman's fine generosity I want
a specific measure of respect returned for the hand
and the back that bears away the stalk
as a boy, in illinois
peeled away, in amazement, the yellow, brown lined case
                              thicker place
when the arced phenomenon
was first put in his hand
a suggestion and a food, combustion!
keep your fingers from the coffee bush.

                                        Nor,
on the meseta Basáltica, or back in town
in Paso de Indios
can the people be permitted
the luxurious image of Peron
and his duly wedded saint
they can be taught to deny
the dictator and his call girl
in the sports car
hide themselves in some corrupt
rooming house country
with a blue coast
and damned clergy

          "memory, mind, and will
              :politics
       "there are men with ideas
        who effect"

Force those men.
be keen to pass beyond all known use
use the grain on a common mountain
for those who are hungry

                    treat hunger
as a ceremony
be quick to pass by condition
and the persuasion of mere number
            teach the parrot, who rises
                        in the sunset
            a cloud
            to sing,
destroy
        all talking parrots
    I ask you
        make for the
                        altar
            of your imaginations
            some sign   Keep
        the small clerks of God from your precinct
be not a world, and therefore halt
before the incursions of general infection
                from a stronger world,
        dance,
                and in your side stepping
                        the spirit
                            will tell where.

FOR THE NEW UNION DEAD IN ALABAMA

The Rose of Sharon
            I lost in the tortured night
of this banished place
    the phrase
        and the rose
        from wandering

away, down the lanes
in all their abstract directions
a worry about the peninsula
of the east,
and the grim territories
of the west
here in the raw greed
of the frontier my soul can find
no well of clear water
it is pressed
as a layer
between unreadable concerns,
a true sandwich, a true
grave, like a performance
in an utterly removed theater
is a grave, the unreachable action makes
a crypt
of distance,
a rose of immense beauty
to yearn for.
the cutting of it
cutting off the world
the thorn however
remains, in the desert
in the throat of our national hypocrisy
strewn we are along all the pathways
of our exclusively gelding mentality
we stride in
our gelding culture.
oh rose
of priceless beauty
refrain from our shores
suffocate the thin isthmus
of our mean land.
cast us back
into isolation

NINE SONGS

1

I will not name her.

    Love takes us
there is no quick way to it
else it is something not proposed
and like an embarrassing gift
always unwrapped under tension
There is where regret is spawned.

    Theory enters my concerns.
Yet I am driven by more casual
intentions,
          and my attention catches all
her firm planned gesture, of sweetness
she misses nothing, tells where I am
in this wilderness.

2

There are each time I talk of it
reflections of my love in her eyes
and there is nothing that fact can surprise
of all the elaboration of whatever syntax
it is within me to devise
can raise her lashes to me, mine
more than what was given of mine to her's.

I told her of all my unavailabilities
in the face of my resistless intentions
and she gazed down with a faint neutral smile.

Where we will go I will take us,
and she will neither say no nor regret
It is I, it is who will forfeit
like an engrossed actuary
all that is not in front of my eyes

3

This afternoon was unholy, the sky
bright mixed with cloud wrath, I read Yeats,
then black, and their land of heart's desire
where beauty has no ebb
                              decay no flood

but joy is wisdom, time
an endless song
                        I kiss you
and the world begins to fade
I kiss you not, the world is not.
I would not give my soul to you yet
the desire inside me burns.
November. The eighteenth was the coldest
this season, encumbered with routine errands
out past the factory
                        black sulphur
and in the dense checks
of its burdensome smoke the intense yellow tanks,
hooded, there sat a smell of weak death

and we pass these days of our isolation
in our rigidly assigned shelters
heads bent in occupation
a couple of pointless daydreamers
smiles lit and thrown into the breeze,

how artful can love
suffer in the cross streets of this town
marked simply by the clicking railroad
and scratch of the janitor's broom.

4

Red wine will flow
sadly past your lips, and leave
with fullness their parting
october is orange
with desolation
the mountains are abandoned
each winter sunset
to those cruel marks of red
or whole lines of remote ranges
lit of desire for you as they recede

                              toward oregon

Nothing will happen.
The brutality of your frankness
has come to me
inches at a time,
and so slowly the pain marches
through the veins of my soul
with the heavy step of a migrating herd
tramping out the vintage
Evening is
              that closing part
of you I sometimes hum as a song to myself
looking down the street through my fingers
through the wreath of myrtle
                              with which you have embellished
                                  my horns

I call
with the thick weight
in my throat
over your terrain
                    O she is a small settlement, there
she is an atmosphere
and we are above it all
under her white gown
            and against my bare shoulder
snow flakes fall
     a slight scent of ginger
  fresh in the wind
of our trip to Knossos

5

Ginger is the color of your eyes and lips
and your voice has all of that spice
in it, it is sad
the tentative color you will know
it does lead the sentences
into the tunnels that comprise
your glance
            and all those mock sincerities
your treacherous nature can contrive.

There are faiths worth five minutes
and no conceivable, save momentarily,
committments to be honored.
                              I say
I will risk everything, risk undue
and you will say I don't know you.

6

The time passes by the count of the contracting leaves
not so much what falls but all falling
from their limbs

                        minute by minute as the days pass on.
All the blocks
of this small city are square. In the rush
of that silent traffic are you

                        there is no way to tell,
afraid to call, to be seen
there is in the eye of the civil world that catch
one kind, one chance to play out the limited numbers
of love and of plausible instances

                        there are
thin possibilities. I am sorry
I push things so far.
        The afternoon, although the lowness of the sun
is true in november, bright the day is
        of our love
            bright
                our
                    knowledge
    and who does drink far too fast
        of all of it

7

That this is a circle
I never doubted
Look. Men mill
in the corridors of our earth
their moments of loneliness
have left a glistening residue
among its rocks. Say
you love me my precious light
say you do

8

Upon the shore of our world
there appeared one day
an unhappy coincidence
of natures born but not meant
for each other. And no more
was said. No more intended.
There is bred a dark hurt, now
we are at this pass in our mountains
all we had expected, all we had
made secure no matter we missed
it was routine. My Gods
trap and they slay
they pretend to know nothing of frivolity
while their whole pleasure is instruction
in that quality

9

      The first moment

was decisive, it is
in all ways that, trees
are kept to their shedding
if they are of that order
men and women cling together
with the utmost labor
you must
grant me predictions
beyond your simple means.

Two ages come together
for measures of what
is interesting in them
there is that allegiance
of curiosity
          and fire

but beyond that
there is nothing of cognizance
each treats the other as slow-witted
and both are
there was an exchanged thrill
in our glances
but you will remember
a different thing when you are older
than I shall or do now.

    Your recollection likely
will be an interlude
of diverting smiles
and mine will have been keen desire
which is simply the vicious
clinging to that initial of all life
the one undiminishable residue
from the first shock of light
and sustained by the long passion for darkness
man is.
Rather stupid.

    These states waste
so much in ways
who could guess
                    Why speak?
and why to you in particular.
I didn't care for you
at all, there were *only*
those moments I spoke of
as intense pain
which could be any form
of desire, which I wanted
as a possibility made real
and removed to a time
more plausible for myself.

This is what I say
because I despise unaccountable
behavior, any exchange
that puts me down
not that you loved me
but why did you say?
nothing, all tricks ruled out.

I can't honestly think
more of it, if the moon
were more interesting
one could do more than look
at it
consider it else than a device
an ornament, a revolutionary fixture
caught by a simple
and preordained misappointment
but you knew that love
taken into the interior of cold,
northern places is a temptation
of heat and literal rooms
beyond any alternate excitement
and how unaccountably slow it dissolves.
You knew how you turned
my whole attention when other claims
some hesitating moments in the street
a view of white mountains
a task of the senses not performable
and which, for fear of destruction
I would not recall its image.

Goodbye in honor of several things
left undone.

ON THE NATURE OF COMMUNICATION
SEPTEMBER 7, 1966

As Dr. Verwoerd one day
sat at his appointed desk
in the parliament at Capetown
there came to him a green
and black messenger.
(who did not, in fact, disagree with him)

and Dr. Verwoerd looked up
as the appropriately colored man
approached. He expected
a message. What he received
was a message. Nothing else.

That the message was delivered
to his thick neck
and his absolute breast
via a knife
that there was a part tied
to the innate evil of the man
is of no consequence
and as the condolences, irrelevant.

Thus, in the nature of communication
Dr. Robert Kennedy is deeply shocked
and Dr. Wilson shocked
Dr. Portugal, that anonymous transvestite
is "with" the gentle people of
South Africa in this their moment
                of grief
                and wishes them well

in their mischief. A practical
and logical communication. Pope
Johnson also deplored etc.
Dr. Mennen Williams said something about "africa."

By its nature communication
ignores quality and opts for accuracy:
come on, tell us how many nigger's balls
tonight. Do not fold bend spindle or mutilate,
I needn't tell anyone
who has received a paycheck,
is each man's share in the plan.

WAIT BY THE DOOR AWHILE DEATH,
THERE ARE OTHERS

Is this the inch of space in time I have
I awoke just now
I don't know from what
I could suppose a certain gas
                    it could have been
        thinking of myself

Is this thing made
with the end built-in
the component of death hidden only
in the youthful machine
but discoverable if the wrench
                    of feeling

is turned near forty when the doors
shut with a less smooth click
and biological deliquescence
a tooth broken and unrecoverable
ah news from the Great Manufacturer.

This afternoon someone, an american
from new york, spoke
to me knitting his brows, of
"the american situation" like
wasn't it deplorable, a malignancy
of the vital organs say News
from nowhere. A mahogany sideboard of tastes.
I knitted my brows too
an old response
        and tried to look serious
Look like I was thinking of quote back home.

Look like I *have* a home, pretend
like anyone in the world
I know where that is. And could
if I chose, go there.

I thought sure as hell
he is going down
the whole menu

                Civil rights cocktail
                Vietnam the inflexible entree

oh gawd what will there be for pudding
(not another bombe

I shifted deftly out the window
of the new university, the english workers
saunter easily building this thing.

    What has been my stride
My body remains younger
than I am. I let part of my beard grow
in September and touching it

with my hand when I turned in bed
I woke up. Hair on the face is death
it is that repels the people gets
a sociological explanation. Disaffection
is in our day the fear of death
the bare face is thought permanent,
a rock. But not clean.
The cat is cleaner when he licks
his hair and claws following a meal.

I nearly died the other day, without intention.
And when I thought Death had come for me
before My Time I was in a fright
to know what to do last
in what city to meet my gunner Meg
be beside me
            and laughed
like a tired runner at the end of hurrying.
            It was dry.
The laughter a hiss at environment.
And just now, reconsidering this
I hear the crows, I have
not seen augurous birds since we moved
away from the rookery in Lexden churchyard
they rise with the dawn now and flutter
in hoarse astonishment
around the top of the sycamore in the garden
the mists from the North Sea move rapidly by.
The wind rushes and turns. "A blackening train
Of clamorous rooks thick urge their weary flight.

I have no more sense of death than
the intimations the starlings
bring and no cold wish to be there
in that place. The rot of finger tips
and an old fern grown full inside my skull
are the passing, dull
presentments I have.
I have felt already the reality

of the last breath I draw in.
I want to say something.
                    I want to talk
turn myself into a tongue

It was a short exhalation
rose from me as the smoke
from a blown out candle
thick with the first vacuum
then suddenly thin, the intention
of a whisper and smile.

The question of the child
"what is it" is only possible
from the neuter distance of the child
when a stranger walks alone
far out on the quay
or, as there are no estuaries
where I come from
across an open field

The crossection of the monument of Death
involves the shadow of
the rushing spider
when it is crushed
but the intersection of the moon
is absolute
    the human presence
        and the power to be
            is that small
        our time and
            place
                is that limited
                    our cry for god
        that weak
            our religion
                    that constructed

There was a Saturday gathering
of people
Stones outside shop near Pound's
london residence, Kensington walk
a mews. My dream
had me pound stone. A woman agent
of the university of texas was there
didn't meet her, and another awful creature

from new york.
We drank small glasses of bubbly wine
said to be from Spain, tasting suspiciously
morocco. Headstone.

            How we inscribe our days
to boredom. The next week I sat
while a harmless collagist
drew my portrait.
But I was bored past the threat of
Death. It took a double shot of whiskey
in Liverpool street to revive me.

It is difficult enough to sit still for love
and now the price of the time for that
rises like the hem, or goes down
as some predictable opposite. April
is my month. I learn the 6th card
of the major arcana. But so is March
the zodiac cuts me that way, the ram
and the bull, it is love I am
or the 5th, and mediate the material
and divine, a simple sign   the ram
the reflection of Isis. I wear
a tiara. I can think of people
who won't believe that.
                        The body. I am
however, the host of my body.
I invite myself to enter myself.
I have gone there sometimes with great pleasure.

We are not in God's name. At the end,
when the dreaming of the dream
came I "thought" I was Sophia Loren
a mature venus. I don't resemble her.
She could be Mama Courage.

In God's name I do not seek an end.
The imitation of life is more vivid
                    than life
                            (Paul, here is your
                                    name
                            as cool as anything

So there is a dream story
    of a true enough man named Pedro
"a man without a country"
in the cowering simplicity of the newspaper phrase
it is reported he was a stowaway
on the English cargo ship Oakbank 2 years ago
but he has no papers and every country
rejects him. He says he is Brazilian.
He will ply the seas, a captive there
until he dies. His references do not exist.
No Deans will welcome him. No housewives
have come forth with a cup of coffee
no workers will welcome him upon the job
no greeting of any kind seems forthcoming.
He shall ply the seas until he dies.
His references do not exist. Notice.
No one will recommend him. His first name
is all he has, always the sign of
an acutely luckless man, his first name
can be used by anyone, indeed only
his first name, the excuse for abandoning him
is complete. Even the crew of the Oakbank
I should imagine
are waiting for the day he, idling about the ship
washes over and saves them the handling
of his body against the rail and into the foam

where he at last must be and even now is
as he walks the decks, no nation possesses
the apparatus to fix another identity
or any identity for this man who is without one.
He is the man we all are and yet he doesn't exist.
He is the man we would all save with our tongues
because we are secretly him. His references of course
do not exist. He may recall as we do
the uncertain days on shore
when they did, when once, remember that time
the world seemed open what a satisfying meal
that was. The body outlives
in Pedro too, its lighted parts. The rest
is application, qualified and eager young man
or woman, fluent french and english
would travel . . .

A NOTATION ON THE EVENING
OF NOVEMBER 27, 1966

The moon is a rough coin tonight
full but screened by lofty moisture
bright enough to make sure
of the addresses
on the letters I drop in the red pillar box
Frost is on the streets. A soft winter breeze
comes from the North Sea into my nostrils
I am at home here only in my mind
that's what heritage is.
Turning the corner, only our windows
along the ribbon of road are lit
I know my wife has gone to bed
and that the gas is burning
and that my heart and my veins

are burning for home. Yet those abrupt times
I hear the harsh voice of home
I am shocked, the hair on my neck
        crawls.
This evening we all went to see
an old classic flick at the Odeon
The magnificent seven introducing
Horst Buchholz, I'd seen it before
and *had not* got it that a german
played a mexican, of course!
An American foreigner is every body
navajoes play iroquois
the American myth is only "mental" a foreigner
is *Anybody*. Theoretically at least
an Italian could play
an English man or a London jew
if nobody knew.
Tom and Jenny were there
and Nick Sedgwick.
Tom remarked, on the evidence of
the last scene when the Mexican-
Japanese said Vaya con Dios
and Yul said a simple adios.
"that was philosophical."
Then the five of us went home
singing Frijoles!
twirling our umbrellas
and walking like wooden legged men in a file
one foot in the gutter
        the other on the sidewalk.

EXECUTIONER, STAY THY COLD BLADE

As knowledge grows
it becomes apparent
that the brain
is a machine
of a type
very different
from those made hitherto
by the thotfull
   efforts of man

Its success is largely due
to the richness
of its parallel circuits
and its redundancies

This makes it very difficult
to assign particular functions,
especially
by the technique of removal

SONG

Again, I am made the occurrence
Of one of her charms. Let me
Explain. An occupier
Of one of the waves of her intensity.

One meeting

Behind the back
        of the world
Brief and fresh
And then
Nothing.
Winter nights
The crush of fine snow
A brilliancy of buildings around us
Brief warmth
In the cold air, the cold temperament
Of a place I can't name

    Now what is it. Turning into
A shadowed corridor half the earth away
And deep inside an alien winter
I remember her laugh
The strange half step she took

        And I would not believe it
If Europe or England
Could in any sense evoke her without *me,*
The guitar of her presence the bearer of her scent
Upon my wrist
The banding of her slightsmiling lassitude . . .

THE SUNDERING U.P. TRACKS

I never hear the Supremes
but what I remember Leroy.
McLucas came
to Pocatello the summer of 1965
one dark night he was there
in a brilliant white shirt, one
dark evening the U.P.
brought him, the most widely luminous
and enchorial smile
      I ever saw.
              He had taken rooms
with the Reverend Buchanan
over in that part of town owned
by Bistline, the famous exploiter.

I was hurt to discover he had come
to what I thought was my town in my fair country
three days before. I had thought
he would stay with me.
How many thousand years too late now
is that desire. How long will the urge to be
remain. Every little bogus town
on the Union Pacific bears the scar
of an expert linear division.

              The rustic spades
              at the Jim Dandy Club
              took his money
              like sea winds lift
              the feathers of a gull

     "Compared to the majestic legal thievery
of Commodore Vanderbilt men like Jay Gould
and Jim Fisk were second-story workers . . ."

(rest comfortably Daniel Drew)

Each side of the shining double knife
from Chicago to Frisco
to Denver, the Cheyenne cutoff
the Right of Way they called it
and still it runs that way
right through the heart
the Union Pacific rails run also to Portland.
Even through the heart of the blue beech
hard as it is.

> 2000 miles or so
> each hamlet
> the winter sanctuary
> of the rare Jailbird
> and the Ishmaelite
> the esoteric summer firebombs
> of Chicago
> the same scar tissue
> I saw in Pocatello
> made
> by the rapacious geo-economic
> surgery of Harriman, the old isolator
> that ambassador-at-large

You talk of color?
Oh cosmological america, how well
and with what geometry
you teach your citizens

THE OCTOPUS THINKS WITH ITS ARMS

Out of the total of some 500 million nerve cells
300 million and more are in the arms

The script in the memory
does not include the recognition of oblique rectangles

In the optic lobes of an octopus
we meet the first great sections of the visual computing system
a Mass of 50 million neurons behind each eye

The optic lobes themselves can be regarded as the classifying
and encoding system and as the Seat of the Memory

The male Octopus Vulgaris fucks by putting the tip
of his third arm
inside the mantle of the female
who sits several feet away
looking like Nothings Happening for about a half hour

The females are impregnated before they are mature
the spermatophores survive until the eggs are ripe
Both animals are covered with vertical stripes during their session
and move not at all.

THE HISTORY OF FUTURES

The long horn was an automotive
package of hide & bones, a few hundred
pounds of dope which delivered itself
entirely free of moral inconvenience
known otherwise as fat
yet with a memory fresh enough to market

The Bloody Red Meat Habit
dates from about 1870
Before that we were a Sowbelly Nation
feeding off the wisest of the omnivores
Beef is the earliest element
of the crisis, a typical texas imbalance

Importations, trash beef from Argentina
are meant to satisfy
the Bloody Red Meat Habits
of our best friends, and in fact
as pet lovers secretly understand
you Can fool fido

With Foodstamps we have pure script
the agricultural subsidy farmers have enjoyed
under every name but socialismo
since World War II

Which brings us
to a truly giant dog named Ronald
the most immense friend conceivable
a Fenrir created by beef heat
and there you have your bullshit apocalysis

One morning, in his mythological greed
He swallows the Sunne

[for my students at Kent State
 Spring, 1973]

THE STRIPPING OF THE RIVER

The continental tree supports the margins
In return for involuntary atrophos
Which can now be called the Shale Contract
Not only are the obvious labors
In metal and grain and fuel extracted
But the spiritual genius is so apt
To be cloven from this plain of our green heart
And to migrate to the neutralized
And individualizing conditions of the coasts
That this center of our true richness
Also goes there to aberrant rest
Bought by the silver of sunrise
And the gold of sunset.

VICTORIO

There is a season of gold
before the energy of a people
comes to its ritual close
and this is a metaphor not satisfied
by the mines

There is no call
to mourn the death of Victorio
he was spared the trivial meanness
of imprisonment and slavery
No principles generated
by a moral quandary in time
and in fact Apache heads
were rather amused by Oklahoma

See the pictures of Geronimo's band
riding in dormant automobiles
or holding the biggest pumpkin

Yet his taste for Death
is the Bitterness we find on the tongue
when we consider La Gran Apacheria

He is the most dreaded
The most terrible
The most famous

NANA & VICTORIO

Along this spine of dragoon mountains
the pains in Nana's bit off leg
a wound inflicted by the vicious teeth
of the Alien Church, their thin line
moves north then south
across the rio bravo del norte
the winde driving the wild fire of their loyalties
and in the cruel vista
I can see the Obdurate Jewel
of all they wanted, shining
without a single facet
upon our time
and yet the radiance marks everything
as we unweave this corrupted cloth

DRESS FOR WAR

Tallow shampoo so the hair is sleek & obedient
Vermilion for the face and Blue micaceous stone
    whose dust glitters weirdly
From a conejo deer an inch wide band of blood
    from ear to ear
Copperore for green stripes
The best army field glasses
    with which to sweep Hades

The most absolute of the predatory tribes
Apache policy was to extirpate
Every trace of civilization
From their province

GERONIMO

We call his mother Juana
She had him near Tulerosa
Rocket Country still
Notorious through his opposition
To Alien authority
And by Systematic
And Sensational advertising
His Pleasures were widely known
As Depredations
Among the Invader

Eyes like two bits of obsidian
With a light behind them

JUH & GERONIMO

Friends from boyhood
In Chihuahua and Arizona
Perfecting their senses
In the portable forge of summer
Got down to the Mother Mountains
Their obsessive democracy
Blown out at the points of control,
Crazy with permission
A noiseless ecstasy
Only they can hear
Each man permitted
More than a man can bear
Against the true as steel
Military Republicanism
Of the Norte Americanos

NANAY

Great hardness in old age
He can be imagined
Straight from the flaking slopes

A strong face
Marked with intelligence
Courage
And good nature, but
With an understratum
Of cruelty and vindictiveness

He has received many wounds,
    muchas gracias amigos
In his countless fights
With the whites,
    muchas gracias amigos

In each ear it was his pleasure
To wear a huge gold watchchain

SHIFTING AN INTERFERENCE WITH NATURE
TO A SCIENTIFIC OBSTRUCTION

Humming birds are close to junkies anyway
All that keeps them straight is the flower
And her control of plenitude in their cause
Curbing their overweening gluttony
And their insatiable singlemindedness
Yes, as the books say, they are pugnacious
But in them it is a quality absolutely without wit.

So when this normality is disturbed
And they go for sugar in water and acid red #27 [a]
They do get vicious as the supply gets low
And at this point Harmonics drive these hovercrafters
Crazier still as it punctuates their slavery[b]
And their birdbrained anger spreads
Throughout their frenzied holding patterns
Sugar, sugar

a. Index number for red #2
b. An experiment conducted at 110 degrees fahrenheit
   scale (a mere 70 degrees below the fundamental
   interval) by Jeremy Prynne, using the upper registers
   of a # 365 Marine Band Hohner.

AN OPINION ON A MATTER OF PUBLIC SAFETY

Air Bag sounds like eminent sickness
This device should not be permitted
General Motors was right to suppress it,
and wrong to have relented
and Nader should stay out of it.

Driving is based on alertness
whether that be loose or tight
Those who let their attention wander
must not be encouraged to survive
by a bag full of air[a].

a. Air bags are a good example of Say's
Law, which says, that production creates,
notoriously, the product, but the market
also. And of course, the rationale, in this
instance, Immortality.

WET CAKES

Did you ever get the impression
standing in the supermercado
that an awful lot of people,
in California, want the *water*
but they'd just as soon skip the rain?

THE SOCIOLOGY OF GAMES

In soccer
when you do something good
you get a hug and a kiss

In american football
when you do something good
you get a slap on the ass.

DEL MAR

Del Mar was the favorite track of J. Edgar
And he used to take along his buddy, Clyde
One can see the golden mason ring glint wahoo
On the snowy Pullman napkin and african waiters
Serving ham & eggs, walkin with the car

They'd be put up in a mansion
Over by the water and their every wish
Taken care of with a catering snap.
Del Mar is a serious track; maybe too serious.

YOU'RE SUPPOSED TO MOVE YOUR HEAD, NOT YOUR EYES

We now live next to the tennis court
Yellow green balls seem to be the thing
this season. For phrases we get
Vicious shot! Or, I *knew*
you were gonna do that!

Last Saturday we watched
the finals, inside. Vilas has got
an arm like a gorilla, and
it appears, it also serves
as his main instrument of thought
since it returns the ball
so often to the same place.[a]

Outside, on our court,
the less consecutive thocks and thucks
labor along on raw audible time
dramatized by the brain's impatience
with bleak, netted balls.

Connor's paranoid study of his strings
reminds the nation that tennis
is the only game in which the instrument
suffers the blame for error.[b]

The chat between the broadcasters
is gruesomely tedious. These people
walked into an upper middle class sport
and they don't know even how to look at it.

a.   A tennis intelligence is subtle up to but not including the shot.

b.   Even the Dentist, that meanest class of sportsman, when he breaks your
     tooth, doesn't exclaim Shit! as he critically stares at his pliers. Footbol,
     both types, is perhaps least dilated by this instrumental paranoia. The
     passer does not glare in hatred at the hand which overthrew the pass, nor
     does the kicker inflict punishment on the foot that missed the goal. The
     hunter does not throw away the gun that missed the duck &c.

PALMS, VICTORY, TRIUMPH, EXCELLENCE

My L.A. began in 1947
when I was in high school
and the derricks were still up.
I was fresh from Illinois
enlightened by Malinowski.

The excitement was not
in The Light, even then
beginning to be obscured
but in the Palm Trees
those companions
of the dinosaurs.

They are as snobbish as ethiopians
in their attitude toward man.
They follow him everywhere
except where it gets uncomfortable.

My favorite palms are in Riverside,
ol'downtown.
When someone told me
they are the preferred dwelling
of rats
I was emphatic in my disbelief
and in my disapproval of the possibility.

But of course, rats are smart.

INDEX OF TITLES AND FIRST LINES

INDEX OF TITLES AND FIRST LINES

Titles of poems are given in Italic type

A NOTE ON THE AUTHOR

Edward Dorn was born in Villa Grove, Illinois, in 1929; and was educated at the University of Illinois and Black Mountain College. He has taught at Idaho State University in Pocatello, the University of Essex, the University of Kansas, the University of California at Riverside and at La Jolla, Kent State University, and the University of Colorado.

His *Collected Poems* and the complete *Gunslinger* were published in 1975, and *Hello, La Jolla* and *Views & Interviews* in 1978.

GREY FOX PRESS BOOKS

Robert Creeley *Was That a Real Poem & Other Essays*

Guy Davenport *Herakleitos and Diogenes*

Edward Dorn *Selected Poems*

Allen Ginsberg *The Gates of Wrath: Rhymed Poems* 1948-1952
Gay Sunshine Interview (with Allen Young)
Improvised on the Tongue

Jack Kerouac *Heaven & Other Poems*

Frank O'Hara *Early Writing*
Poems Retrieved
Standing Still and Walking in New York

Charles Olson *The Post Office*

Gary Snyder *He Who Hunted Birds in His Father's Village: The Dimensions of a Haida Myth*

Gary Snyder,
Lew Welch,
Philip Whalen *On Bread & Poetry*

Lew Welch *How I Work as a Poet & Other Essays/Plays/Stories*
I, Leo—An Unfinished Novel
Ring of Bone: Collected Poems 1950-1971
Selected Poems
Trip Trap (with Jack Kerouac & Albert Saijo)

Philip Whalen *Decompressions: Selected Poems*
Scenes of Life at the Capital